CROSSING

A CAREGIVER'S JOURNEY

LEOTA ESTER

International Standard Book Number 13: 978-1-60452-150-4
International Standard Book Number 10: 1-60452-150-3
Library of Congress Control Number: 2019955016

BluewaterPress LLC
2922 Bella Flore Ter
New Smyrna Beach FL 32168

This book may be purchased online at -
https://www.bluewaterpress.com/crossing

Written by: Leota Ester

Cover illustration by: Jeffrey Woodson

Seasonal illustrations by Camin Potts

A poem begins
as a lump in the throat
a sense of wrong
a homesickness
a love sickness.

—Robert Frost

Preface

The question most asked of me regarding my husband Lee's Alzheimer's Disease has been, "When did you know?" I, nor I suspect anyone who cares for a loved one beginning that journey, can pinpoint a time when we "knew."

It sneaks up. It's not forgetting which we all do, especially as we get older. It's the surprise actions of that loved one, the strange decisions, the unusual and unlikely behavior that causes us to pause and finally say, "Something's wrong."

For example, I said to the neighbor who accused Lee of looking in her window, "No, no, Lee would never do that." She replied, "He did." When he threw rubber tubes, used for floating, on the banks of a nearby stream, I cried out, "Lee, we don't do that." When he took the frozen food that was to go into the freezer in the garage and sat it on the floor, leaving it there to melt, I understood he was changing.

To realize that the one we love can no longer do ordinary things, or be consistent with past behavior, is making strange decisions out of keeping with his or her character is to have clues that these are changes that will require the caregiver also to change. I tried to record both in the poems.

Slowly, however, I learned how to respond to the downward path, recording those many encounters with these poems. They became a story of patient caregiving, being non-judgmental, finding ways to deal with deep and unanswerable questions, using walks, games, books, singing in creative ways, ensuring that friends came to make both Lee's and my days as good as possible. These poems are that story.

Join me on my journey.

Acknowledgements

Among those I want to acknowledge are Wisconsin's first Poet Laureate, Ellen Kort, who with a small writers' group including Alice Baumbach, Amy Bertschausen, Tricia Matthew and Deb Andrews, heard the poems as they were being written and insisted I gather them in a form to share.

In addition I acknowledge with love and appreciation:

My three daughters Jenni, Libby and Mary who lovingly stayed with me as I agonized over the poems, put off getting them into book form and kept saying, "Do it, Mom."

Emily Remillard, my eldest granddaughter, who spent many hours with me reading, sorting, thinking about the poems' messages, selecting, suggesting changes, additions, clarifications, believing in their value.

Susan Woodson, my dear friend, steady and constant companion, who patiently read, made suggestions and encouraged me, and put the poems into usable form for the final steps. Jeffrey Woodson, her son, an industrial designer, drew the sketch for the cover.

For those final steps, I gratefully acknowledge Camin Potts for her guidance through the printing process, selection of style, final presentation and book design.

Friends Lowell and Mary Peterson and their daughter, Kitty O'Callaghan each made a needed and significant contribution as a published author sharing knowledge, a friend always present, and an editor.

Last but not least, David Hipschman, who would not let me rest until I arranged to contact Joe Clark, publisher and owner of BluewaterPress LLC, New Smyrna Beach, Florida, to complete this work.

Lee

Spring

The Broom

Why is it so hard to find the broom?
The broom
in the closet
right behind you
the broom
on the nail in the closet
the broom
behind the door
where you are standing.
You know
the broom.

No   you no longer know.

Who Am I

You leaned over the bed from your side
to get as close to my face as possible
looked for a little while
finally said
"Am I your son? I am your son, aren't I?"

No   you married me
I'm your wife
we walked down the aisle
the day we were married
smiling
surrounded by all those friends.

Remember?
You're my husband.

Blank Smiles

Where have you gone?
We stand before the mirror
both looking into it
you shaving cream on your face
me curling my hair
I stare
I think about the young man I fell
in love with
the middle-aged man who wrote
news stories
served on committees
sang in the choir
fathered our children
but they have gone
no longer here.

Nevertheless
I see a smile
I smile back.

Helping

You sleep
you had kissed me
twice
"good night."

As I gathered pop   beer   chips
frozen enchiladas from the freezer
put them in the cooler
for tomorrow's trip
to the cottage
as I
shook out the rug
made sticky rolls
filled the dishwasher
you slept.

You say
you would have helped
but   it's no longer help.
I let you sleep.

Surprise

I keep thinking that you do know
what you are doing
then I see you step into the shower
naked
except for the black sock
half off
half on
toe flapping about
as you begin to wash yourself.

Too Far to Remember

Four pair of underwear
on the edge of the dining room table
remind me again
that you no longer do the simplest tasks
from the basket
at the bottom of the steps
to the drawer in your room
is too far
for you to remember
what you started to do
you laid them on the table.
Most of us
lay something down
forget
but seeing it later
remember
finish the job
I may wish that you could do that
but
you no longer can.

I say nothing
I understand.

Taking Out the Garbage

No   I remind myself
don't ask.
A couple of months ago
or even just a month ago
I could have asked you to do a simple task
you might have said yes
and forgotten
but when you remembered
you would have done it
then later
as it became harder to remember
we did our chores together
making sure we put out the garbage
checking to see the garage door was down
now
you watch "The Forsythe Saga"
and I slip away
as you
unaware that I have left
sit   safe in your chair.
Just to be able to balance yourself
is quite enough
without a load of garbage in your arms
or the papers   cans   bottles
for tomorrow's pickup.

You would help
but I can't let you.

"Where Are My Keys?"

Dressed in coat   hat   earmuffs
you moved anxiously about the room
leaned over the dresser
searching for your keys
wandered about the living room
peered into the wastebasket
behind the couch
looked on the kitchen counters
grew agitated.
"Where are my keys?" you demanded.
I rose from my chair
stopped in the bathroom
for a moment while you paced
said "We'll find them"
checked the key rack
thought for a minute
put my hands in the pocket
of the big fat coat you wore
drew them out
put them in your hands.

You said "Oh."
I hugged you.

Alone

You're more confused than usual
getting dressed took a couple of hours
even Zoom
your favorite cereal
couldn't move you
to change out of your pajamas
shave
brush your teeth
going to the Y didn't call to you
as it usually does
eager to get away
be on your own
you sat   looked at your socks
motionless
finally pulled at one of them
then sat some more.

Was there too much to think about
did having to make a choice
slow you down to this inertia
does worry
lock your movement?
You can't tell me
or let me reassure you
I don't know what is on your mind.

We are both alone.

What Purpose, the Tests?

I'd rather not, another time, Doctor,
bother to have tests done
to see if my husband has Alzheimer's.

I don't need you to point to words
to see if they can be repeated
hold up lines of different shapes
to see if they can be matched.
Why do you care
What will you know
What will you do with these? I ask.
"When you come back
five years or so
this baseline will be handy.
We'll be ready to compare."

Five years?
It's today that I live with...
where is he
what will he buy
when will he return
will he fall
pee in the bed
eat too much
take too much medicine
wander out undressed.

Notes on your paper filed in your records
statistics for a later date are no help.
What am I to do today?

Writing Poetry

You wanted to go to the poetry workshop with Ellen
to write some poetry
to find words
to say something
she suggested
write your name
and you did
then
where you are from
who do you love
what do you fear?
It was too hard
that much you couldn't do.

For the first time
I saw it
your inability to form words
the misspelling of my name
scrawled letters
running at random.

Later during her talk
you clenched your fists
slammed them down on the table
you had wanted so much
to write some poetry
had something you needed to say.

I could only wonder what.

Outside Waiting

You've gotten up
I lie in bed
wait
you close the bathroom door
it's a long time
I hear movement and
I wait
I want you to have privacy
to have some time to call your own
at least in the bathroom
still
I get out of bed
stand outside the door
wonder
listen
try to figure out
could you floss that long
be unable to get the shaving cream out of the can
be on the stool
what do you do so long?

Finally
I call out
"Are you all right?"
You answer
wearily
"I'm all right."

Are you tired of me worrying?
Just as I am.

Thinking Is Hard Work

You stand over the sink
holding your razor
looking at me
struggling to answer my question.
I sit on the edge of the tub
asking
if you enjoyed having Teddy and Larry
to dinner last night
unmoving
staring
not seeing me
you seemed to want to talk
to say something
answer
finally found the words
"Not really."

I felt certain that would be the answer
coming from
deep within the centers of your brain
where the real you still lies
I wondered if you could find it
you did
hard as it was.

Is asking
finding answers
still important for you
or just for me?

Summer

Morning

Stoop down
pick up everything
put it all away
close the cupboard door
lift the pillows from the floor
check to see your clothes are laid out
remove the potholder from the chair
test the water hot enough not too cool
make sure between the toes is dry
snap the pad tightly
toss wet pajamas in the clothes chute
remake the bed
open the windows for fresh air
smile
tease about shaving
"You'll be beautiful   or at least smooth."
zip the zipper on your pants
get the belt in all of the loops
go out to the garage with the old pads
wash another load.

It's every morning
the day has begun.
I try to remember that many others
are doing the same.

That helps.

Waving in the Breeze

It was a mistake
to ask you why you weren't dressed
to hurry you.

Downstairs the door to the patio
slammed
I heard you shouting.

Running down the steps
I was there to see you
looking out
at your Hanes undershorts
where in frustration you had thrown them.
On the limb of the nearby tree
swinging
back and forth
back and forth
too far away to retrieve
they hung for days.

We laughed
the only thing to do.

Stumbling

The man on the street looked up   startled.
You had wobbled precariously
lost your balance
almost fallen
with the sacks of blueberries
tomatoes
flowers
that you held in your hands.
He's not drunk
I say   defensively
he's
I pause
unable to say Alzheimer's

old.

Afraid

I'm suddenly afraid.
I haven't been before
you've become noisy
loud
more than ever
constantly
repetitively
very   very   loud
hard on everyone's ears
getting the attention of those around us
making them wonder.
Tonight a man came from another car
to say "Was someone calling for help?"
later I called out to a couple turning to see
what was the source of the loud call
"It's ok   he's all right."
When might they not believe me?
how much does it disturb these strangers
cause them concern?
can it help for them to know that victims
of a nasty disease called Alzheimer's
can be
want to be out   about
in company of others?

I don't ask myself "Is it really ok?"
instead   I know it is
a learning time for everyone.

Let the Questions Go Unasked

I forget what I know
not to ask you questions
when they no longer can be answered
nothing can come of them.
"Why wouldn't you stay in the bathroom
until you are dressed?"
"Why do you wander through the house naked?"
"Where did you put the mail?"
"Why aren't you ready yet?
are questions that have no answers
as hard as you may try.
But I can see
they leave a hurt inside you
hovering
unrelieved.

They sadden you.

Looking for Answers

You remain silent after I ask
"Do you want to go to Roger's church or ours?"
I almost slap my forehead for forgetting
not remembering that I have learned
not to ask you to make a decision
you no longer can
but wanting to honor you   I've asked.
After a period of quiet time
you suddenly say in a quiet voice
"I don't care which church we go to."
Then I ache   that
while able to finally answer
you no longer care.
So much has gone   the loud response
the calling out the name of a sign we pass by
the ever-present "Ahhing"
your ability to know and understand
being able to make up your mind.

Are these permanent signs of Alzheimer's
or might you be all right again
if I could find the perfect medication
a tried and true exercise program
the right diet
could you heal   be continent
answer my questions   talk to me?

Have I done enough?
Could I do more?
No one seems to know.

Elwood

Elwood leaned across the kitchen table
looked you in the eye
told you when the Caddis flies
would swarm above the river
when fish would jump
asked if you had a bamboo fly rod
watched you try to find words
to answer
saw you struggle to understand.
He knew something was wrong
but even so
he stayed with the conversation
giving you
talk you needed
pretend conversation
as if it were real.
Few can do that now
most turn to talk to others present
change their directions
shift their chairs
act as if you were
no longer there.

Elwood stayed with you.

Vacuuming

You vacuumed.
The Asian beetles caught your eye
immediately
as we entered the guest room of the cottage
"Ahhhhhhh," you cried out   pointing.
I said, "You need to vacuum."
You did
you vacuumed
vacuumed
vacuumed
over and over
over
over
getting every beetle
finding yet another
crying out "AAAHHHHH"
pointing
moving to it   vacuum cleaner in hand
with purpose and determination.
How many times did you go over the floor
over and over
over
over?

I neither know nor care
You were so happy.

One More Thing to Do

You slept all night
rose   dressed   slept again
leaning with your head in your hands.
You slept
head falling back on the pillows of the couch
still you slept on
legs stretched out before you
mouth open
gone to the world
still you slept
your eyes opened   looked about
fell shut again
no snoring now.
Hours pass
until I shake you   say
"We're going home. We need to leave the cottage."

I pack quickly
roll curtains down
make sure the burners on the stove are off
ease you to the car
your arms over my shoulders
your body loose and wavering.
Home unpacking
I see two days' medicine   not one   gone
let you sleep this out.

Frightened   I know
you can no longer
give yourself your medicine.

Going to the Movies

A few couples sit scattered in the darkened theater
watching   listening
to the story of Howard Hughes
as he climbs to his dream
of flying faster than anyone
being the richest in the world
despite obsessions with germs
his personal fears.
I watch you from the corner of my eye
to see if you too listen
are caught up in the story
you seem to be
you look intent
lean forward
I turn back to the story
munch my popcorn.
Then as Hughes shouts out an order to his men
you shout along with them
"OK!"
I pat your knee
knowing now for sure
you get the story
wait to see if you will
once again
lose yourself in the movie.
You do.
Do I care if those about us hear your
next loud reply to Howard's question
your "NO!"?

Never.

Book Club

The discussion of the book over
the meat grilled
potato salad eaten
talk turned to chatter
while doing dishes together
instructions shared about building a deck
how to find local workmen
goes on behind us in the cottage
friends together on a summer day
by the lake.
We sit
you and I
outside on the deck
where you are not lost in the laughter and talk.
I lean in
sit close
making sure you feel
we chose this spot
the place we wanted to be.
I create a conversation
of our own
about the choppy water
a slowly moving speed boat
the crushed, or is it rotted, stone on the paths
the lemonade.

Together   apart   alone.

Another Moment

Two booths in the restaurant had occupants
one held a man slowly eating a piece of pie
in the other a mother and daughter
sat staring at one another.
I said to you
"While we may find a bit of fault with Patrick's hair,
what about the "do" on the girl who just came in?"
Sticking out in all directions
carefully coiffed
it had caught your eye too.
Still able to see   be non-judgmental
to smile at what seemed an absurdity
to old eyes
you seemed to understand
our aging attitude.
To catch you still aware
to see that smile of recognition
to share a moment
for that short time
I had you with me.

Better yet
you had you.

Tenderness

We drive down the busy street towards town
I with one hand on the wheel
the other on your thigh
patting
squeezing gently
holding with tenderness.
It's as close as we get these days but it's close.

I'm grateful.

If Only I Had Known

I wish I had known years ago
when we went to Door County to see Joan
that she did indeed know us.
I was sure pretty sure   but then   not sure
she couldn't walk on her own
said nothing
looked at us   tried to smile
ate her supper with Stan's help and we left for home.
Now as sure as sure
I know that when she saw you
she recognized you
as she reached out   touched your hand
wanted to say something.
She knew you.

I wish I had known then what I know now
that you recognize family and friends
even when you cannot say so
I see what it means to you
to have them visit
smile at you   touch you   make you laugh
tell you a story.
I would have told her about our girls
remembered with her
our many family adventures
even though
it might have seemed
she wouldn't remember.

I wish I had known she knew.

Crying

I've only cried
out loud
one time so far
at Libby's
at Christmas
in the laundry room
when
alone with Mike
who
without judgment
let me cry until I could stop.

The Waiting Wail

A year has passed
since you began to change
or is it two
three
still you surprise me
you forget who came to visit tonight
wonder who your daughter is
in the family picture
you fail to finish your lunch
put your clothes away in strange places.
I understand
the tangles in your brain
mess up
your memory
webs grow far too fast
take away your reason
your grasp of life
make talk impossible
create confusion and despair.

The unshed tears
lie deep inside me
waiting for that time when I can wail.

When Do We Know?

Dear Luella,

I sit by the window with the cold gray sky lined
with pale rose and light blue behind the cold rising
gray smoke of the paper mills in the flats by the river. A
couple of flags, tattered from the winds, flap vigorously
from south winds. blowing bitter cold in January.

A semi, its bed wrapped in gray cloth covering,
passes on the bridge. Then a Fed Ex truck passes, a
white van, a green van, all getting about the day's
business this early Monday morning. Lee sleeps. Or
was sleeping. I hear the heavy sigh that often marks his
presence and will leave the writing for another time.

I don't know how much he knows of his own
illness, slowing down, or, more accurately, I don't know
if he has named his slowing down Alzheimer's. I think
so. I don't think so. It is the same with me. I can and
must. I can't.

At the Food Pantry several weeks ago, having sat
out in the car waiting for him to get the food to deliver,
thinking that I owed him that much regard for his
ability, I went in for the first time and found the people
there kind, but frantic, wondering how to deal with his
confusion. I had no idea that they were experiencing
his difficulty knowing just what he was to do, keeping
things straight and yet, they were uncertain what to do,
when to call, were waiting for me to come.

I, "the last to know" did know, but didn't know;
I understand now about wives who "don't know, but
know," families of abusers who "know but don't know."
I knew, but I couldn't believe that either I, or others,
knew what I knew.

About the same time, he worried about shopping for another person's groceries. When should he do it? How would he find out what he needed? Remembering that he had shopped for a chef a few years ago, I told him the man had died. No, Lee was certain, he needed his shopping done. Checking with the woman at the front desk of the Red Cross, I learned, "Yes, David had died a couple years earlier." The question, asked, opened the door for them to say, "We have been waiting for your call."

Ending the delivery of food to the six women he had taken groceries to for the past years, the shopping for those needing help was difficult for him, for me. The lovely people at the Red Cross seeing my tears as we said good-by called, later. They'd have a cake and punch party for Lee to say thanks and good-by.

The changes have taken a toll not only on him and me, but as well on those called on to reach out, sooth the pain, enable departure gently, be a remembered presence. Thanks again for listening.

Leota

Still Yearning

I want to go on walks we never took
to rivers you haven't fished
to trails we haven't hiked
to Germany where I've never been
to live in different cities for a couple months
learning to know them
as we used to say we would do
when we retired
I want to make time go back
to try again
make those happen
I look at you and believe
for a moment
we can still do it
then stop
think
choose to be grateful
for what is still possible
and memories.

It is enough.

Fall

I Need Your Ready Smile

I've decided that I need to visit you
at least once a day
friends said "Don't do it.
He won't remember anyway."
I tried
I missed a day
and another day
stayed away
so that "you'd get used to it."

This unnecessary separation
was much too heartbreaking
I come every day for my sake
as well as for yours
I don't want to forget you
I need your smile
your "wellllll"
the huge dimpled smile on your face
the slow but certain pushing from the chair
that greets me
when I walk in the door.

I need your ready smile.

What is For Sure

As I wait for someone to unlock the door
see you
sitting on the couch
before the TV
face brightening
glad to see me
I can only guess at what you think
but
believe you are happy that I've come
relieved not to be forgotten.
Nothing is for sure
except
the smile on your face when you recognize me
your eager steps that greet me
the big kiss when I leave
the silent exchange of love
while together.

For sure.

Watching

You watch for me
wait until I come
see me through the curtained windows
your coat is in your arms
you smile broadly
when the bell is answered
the door is opened to let me in
you have expected me.
Are you always there?
Do you watch the window from the couch
only seeming to watch TV
morning   afternoon   night
waiting until I come?
Do you miss me so much
or do you remember me only
when you see me?
What is in your heart
your mind?

What if I could know?
Would it change anything?

Stacking Your Books

You have stacked your books
the pictures from your walls
your robe
blue-checked shirt
Kiwanis medal of honor
your plaques of recognition
the Torch Award
all neatly piled together
ready to go home.
"I hate this place"
you cry out loud
to me when I come in
and then again
louder
I talk a bit
hang the pictures back on the walls
put little ones on the shelves
hang your clothes in the wardrobe
hug you
tease a little about how much better it looks
now that things are back in place
take you for a walk outside
talk about the fading colors on the tree
sing   we always sing.
Back inside
I don't take you home
I take you to your dinner.

Leaving
to go home alone
sadness overwhelms me.

Again and Again

Men take things off the walls
stacking them
for some reason no one knows
women often pack their clothes
piling them
sorting
ready to go.
Some like you do both
so when I enter your room
I see pajamas books anniversary cards,
handkerchiefs toothbrush
family pictures
in random heaps
mixed up   helter-skelter.
What's in your mind?
I want to ask you   but don't.
When you say "NO"
I leave the piles for others to rearrange
other times you watch   maybe help
as things get put back in place
no "right" place
just a place
where you can begin again
tomorrow
to stack.

Why Am I Here?

Why don't you take me home
you ask
lips turned down in sadness
I say I can't take care of you any longer.
Here
wonderful people care for you
all those folks with legs arms eyes ears hearts
make sure you are safe.
I feel guilty
wonder if you should be home
then stop myself
think of our precious time together
walking hand in hand
taking leisurely long car rides
reading our books
playing simple games
laughing
singing hymns
raking leaves at home
smelling flowers
having dinner.

We kiss good-by
both teary both relieved.

Better Than at Home?

I feel as if I'm begging
I want my friends to reassure me
that what I've done is right
I didn't put you in the Home too soon.
According to Dr. Vogel
"Sooner is better it will give him
time to learn to know the staff
to feel at home   know the routine
be recognized   even loved   adjust.
Entering later   she added
the patient is often confused
unmanageably lost   experiences greater stress."
I rationalized that   alone
I could do nothing more than
wipe up
bend over
tie
untie
feed
turn you
take you to the bathroom
look for you
find you
always unsure
that you were safe.

Was it was the right thing to do?
Or is "to be at home at any cost" best?

Many Hands

We went out to dinner early
time enough to watch a little TV together
in our own home
downstairs
before going back to Brewster Village
you in your chair
me in mine
together for a while.
You rose from your chair
made your "oohing" sound
headed for the bathroom too late.
Shoes untied   retied
pants changed
pad replaced
hands washed
feelings reassured
a reminder
why you live at Brewster Village.

Done over and over
again and again
the endless tasks need many hands.

Stopping By Next Door

I stopped by the Humane Society
to see if you and I could walk over
visit the dogs and cats
just across the street
from Brewster Village
we could meet the dogs and cats
take a treat
learn to know some by name
listen as they bark a welcome
or meow cool indifference
maybe chirp
I don't know
I've never been to the Humane Society before.
Would you like that?
It's close
in the neighborhood
but we've never gone.

Your changing
moving out of ordinary life
my slowing down to join you
has opened doors
we had no time for.

We might have
but didn't think so.

Say "Sure"

You say "NO"
balk
refuse
turn aside
when asked to join the others shredding paper
tearing apart old computer data sheets
cutting coupons
folding plastic bags.
Today
sweet-talked into going to the workshop area
you separate the forms
along the dotted lines
stack them in a pile
for recycling.
I suggest
that tomorrow
instead of saying "NO"
say "Sure."
It's good to be so useful
they like you
remember to say "Sure."
Let's practice it together.

"Sure"
"Sure" you reply.

You Wanted To Go With Me

We stood together in your darkened room
I with my coat on
ready to go home
you with eyes wide and sorrowful
pleading "NO   NO"
in your loudest voice
you didn't want me to go
you held me
hugged me
kissed me
begged me
"Take me with you."
I stayed
took my coat off
sat down and read mail to you
turned on the Prairie Home Companion DVD
we watched.
You reached out and said, "I can't take you."
Such longing
perhaps some understanding.

Pain for both of us.

It's Hard to be an Angel

When I hear all the heroic stories
of those who care for their loved ones
at home
until the very last
I feel guilty
then   try to remember
that without the 24 hour care and love
you get at Brewster Village
I couldn't take you to the movies
find ways to make you laugh
greet you with a smile
be patient when your noises wear
we wouldn't walk in the woods
visit the Paper Museum
go to jazz vespers on Sunday nights
see a movie
I couldn't do it.
If you couldn't return each day to Brewster Village
I'd be too tired
cranky
angry
wasted.
Perhaps I would no longer even like you.

I set aside the stories of other angels
believing finally that
each of us must trust our own wings.

We Have Not Traveled This Road Before

The spring day
the second of April, 2005
came sunny   warm   windless
a good day to pick you up
take you for a ride.
It wouldn't be right to stay inside
on such a day
we went for ice cream
your cone melted
dripped on your blue sweater
we wadded napkins around it
decided not to care
we pressed the button
for the sun roof to open
while we meandered through the countryside
passed old implements stacked behind a barn
saw a man bent over his bushes
looked at a sign proclaiming "organic food grown here"
trees that almost hid a man-made lake
simple country homes.
How could it be
that with all the driving we have done
this road is new to us?
But like so much today   I say
with both surprise and resignation

We have not traveled this road before.

They Ask

Alice came to dinner tonight
she asked about you
I tell her the same stories I have told before
the ones I tell over and over
the one about your going to the movie
shouting an answer to the screen
that when we walk around Brewster we sing rounds
not as rounds but just songs
and that we sing very loudly
I tell her that when friends say "Hello, Lee"
you shout back, "Hellooo, Leee"
I tell the same old stories
new ones take too much energy
to put together
no matter how interesting
they might be
I repeat the stories
because

They ask about you.

Happiness

Mary Ebinger came from D.C. to see you
walked into your room
went directly to your chair
leaned over you   said hello.
I watched her put both hands around your face
stroke you and stroke you again
then put her arms around you
pat you
you patted back
slowly   over and over
both of you patting and stroking
she barely whispering
"Warren says Hi.   Warren says Hi."
Quietly she continued
repeating her hellos
her greetings from Warren
telling you she was glad to see you.
I watched your face grow into a glimmer of surprise
then a glorious smile
finally a beam
you stayed focused on her eyes
yours reaching into hers
hers into yours
she wouldn't let me speak
brushed away my attempt
continued her loving litany.

You
lost in complete attention
glowed with happiness.

Wintering

Friends visit coffee plantations in Costa Rica
golf somewhere in the South
Luella climbs hills in Arizona
We instead walk slowly through the halls
noisy halls of stone
that pretend to be streets
as if in a town when one goes out for a walk
sometimes we dance or
clap our hands to the polka music
listen to Romey play his accordion
sit at our table
move the slot over the called number
until we   too can cry out, "Bingo,"
choose our prize and
try again
or we just walk   even in the cold
outside
on paths around the building
singing
wondering where the birds are
marveling at the piles of snow.

Winter travels of our own.

An Old Friend Called

Bob Clark called last night.
I've never heard of Bob Clark
an old high school friend of yours
who lives in Pennsylvania.
Chuck Lilien had called him
after getting our Christmas letter
to let him know about your health.
Bob wanted you to know
that he remembers you from high school
sat with you at a football game
at the last class reunion
several years ago
wanted you to know he cares about you
just wanted you to know.
I watch your face
look for some recognition
think I catch a glimpse.

I want so much for you to know.

Row Q at the Fox Valley Symphony

I don't like
sitting in Row Q at the PAC
with a friend in the seat
next to me
using the ticket bought for you.
You and I are not here together
as we're supposed to be
listening to the violins
cellos trumpets drums tympani
intent on the music of the symphony
chords notes and counterpoints
but
although I understand that
time has brought you to a place where
you are no longer able to make conversation
during intermission with old friends
are confused by all the people
occasionally burst out aloud with joy at the music
that doesn't
erase the sadness
that you are no longer in Row Q
listening to music
doing what you loved.

I can still be sorry.

Slipping Away

I want to believe that you hear the story
that you understand that in the story I read to you
Elton's Mary is sick.
I hope that you still picture the description
of Mary in her winter coat
huddling for warmth by the blazing stove.
I want you to remember
where we left off when we begin again
yet you are changing.
When I used to capture your eyes
hold you to the story
help you laugh when there was cause
weep with our story friends' losses
I can no longer do that
your eyes are gone to me
they stop for a moment
look at me
then move on to see a passing car
watch those walking by
catch the moving clouds.

Does it matter that I read to you anymore?
Are you   like the clouds   darting in and out
on your way   away?

No Different

When we sit among the residents
of Brewster Village
I wonder again
if I have wronged you
having you here
among the many
who have lost their way
your face has a healthy look to it
you hear my words
you want something
that much I know
even if I don't know what.
Yet
you make your sounds
the last of the pills you were given
hang from your mouth
you no longer clap
when the music ends
it turns out
you aren't more than the others
it's just that I know you
love you
imagine you differently

As you once were.

Dancing

Today
with the others at Brewster
we danced to so-so accordion music
no one cared if it was good music
just loved the sound   the beat.
As we sort-of-waltzed past Joe
he reached out his hands to pat us
Helen from #11
tapped her tennies steadily   on time with the beat.
Bernice asked for "Sweet Georgia Brown"
over and over
a chance to do the Charleston again and again.
you and I with the others
clapped to the beat
crossed our hands on our knees with Bernice
danced by moving our bodies
back and forth
called it the fox trot.

When the program was over
I took you for a ride to Goodwill
to drop off some stuff
then down Wisconsin Avenue   through town.
As I drove about   I sensed   knew
you were happier
hearing the noisy music
in familiar surroundings
with friends who clapped and laughed
who danced in wheelchairs.

All familiar now   comfortable and safe.

"Oklahoma"

I sit beside you
we hold hands   watching "Oklahoma"
in the semi-darkness of your room
you turn to look at me
smile
then look back
we try to sing along
but don't remember the words
you're losing weight
I notice
your hands leave mine
try to reach back for them
hunt for them
yet
your eyes won't leave
the movement on the screen
I say "We liked 'Oklahoma' didn't we?"
you look at me again
turn aside
clasp your head
move it back and forth
close your eyes
then
the smile   the eyes now open
the sudden deep connection
comes   tells me   you do remember.

It's all right to have some pain
remembering.

Staring

Only yesterday it seems
you walked
now you fumble when rising from the chair
lean forward
then backward
wobble
fall abruptly back
you seem to be stuck in that big white chair
watching Joe E. Lewis in an old movie
a video on fly fishing
reruns of The Cosby Show

Endlessly   staring.

Tired

Are you the reason I am so tired
listless   ready to nap at any moment
too weary to phone a friend   write a letter?
I want to blame my heart
sleep apnea
some elusive physical reason for this fatigue
looking for a reason
finding none   I turn to you.
Does it really exhaust me
sap my energy
to drive to Brewster Village
walk through the halls
greet those sitting in the Atrium
ring the bell to let me in
then
sit with you
move slowly through the halls
take the path around the building
by the gardens
smell our rose again
try to have you hear the birds
sing to you   silencing your loud cries
play dominoes
read
stack colored toys
watch Andy and Opie one more time?

I think it might
even as I love you.

Dominoes and Go Fish

We played dominoes today
you won
then we played Go Fish
you won
you liked winning
how strange to have fun
playing Go Fish after all these years
of your not liking games
strange to have slowed down
to such a pace
that we can lean back
relax
match sixes to sixes
sevens to sevens
enjoying this
more than
we could have ever imagined.

Later I started to read from our book.
For the first time
you fell asleep while I read.

Were you tired
bored
has it become too much to ask of you
to do three things?

Blame

Sometimes I think it is my fault
that Lee isn't able to talk   to walk
to be himself.
I did it.
Alzheimer's Disease
came
from my not understanding
what he needed.
If I had just been different
made him happier
had I tried harder.
But
I did try to understand who he was
gave him the best that I could
try to remember   the past   is   past.

We can only live today
give love today.

Yesterdays and tomorrows
don't exist in his world
Why mine?

Don't Change

What happened to our walking?
I thought it wouldn't end
that we could always walk
talking while we walked
not talking really
just me making comments as we walked
we would walk   around the Village
through the halls
into the protected garden
to the front tables and chairs on the lawn.

Today you couldn't walk.
You tried when I begged
but you couldn't stand
your legs weren't steady enough
you bobbed precariously
until I got you in your chair again.

I don't want you to change
I've gotten used to you as you are
I'm not ready for you to change some more.

Christmas 2005

Lights twinkle on the bookshelf over your bed
an amaryllis tries to push some green up at your window
Polar Bear Express and a Tomi de Paola book lie open
the train set from home   stuffed elves
the little old wooden woman dressed in plaid muffler
sit around your room.
On top of your radio that you no longer play
are Christmas cards with pictures on them
letters telling you that friends remember you.
Outside birds peck at the thistle in your bird feeders
inside   somewhere   "Here Comes Santa Claus" plays.
I climb on your lap
listen to your quiet "ahhhs," as I hug you
caress your cheeks
smooth your hair
whisper in your ear.
Your arms around me
tell me that you need these hugs
need to give them back to me.
Words aren't necessary
but how I wish you had them yet
that you could read them   try to speak a few
instead   you give up painfully.
So I read to you poems from our children's old poetry books
look with you at picture books from the library.

Over a year has passed for you in Brewster Village
I watch you disappearing slowly from me
the past fading as each day becomes all that matters
the moment   the quiet time of being
the joyful alive
the peace of the blessed Christmas season.

Lonely and Sad

I can hardly bear to watch the play.
Seeing the two Honkey-Tonk ladies
from the Washy Washy Washateria
playing on the theater stage
becomes unbearable
when I remember you
sitting alone in your room
trapped by your own loudness
to solitude
staring at the TV
waiting for time
for life to pass.

It doesn't feel fair
for me to sit with friends
enjoying the flouncy red dresses,
the belting of the songs.

We are both trapped
lonely and sad.

Winter

Ever Loving

I sit on your lap Lee
when I come into your room.
Settled back in your deep chair
both your eyes and your smile
welcome me
but more than those
your lap.
We snuggle   hug
I rest my face against yours
whisper hello in your ears
smooth your stubbly cheeks.

When I tell others
if they ask how you are
that you are still sweet
that you like me to sit on your lap
that I do
they turn away   embarrassed.

I don't care
I want them to know that love doesn't stop
that hugging is always dear
that even as you slip away
you are you.

March 1961

Forty-four years ago tonight you and I welcomed Mary
our third beloved daughter
Pocatello, Idaho, 1961.
Tonight you remember only with my help
and even then   I'm not sure.
The "YEESSSS" could be remembering
could be just a response
could be nothing but another noise you make
I choose to think you remember
so go on talking about her as a child
swinging in the seat you hung from the branch
watching her big sisters play in the yard
making castles in the sandbox by the Russian Olive tree
lying with her head on Soy the big Siamese
using him for a pillow
loving her four-year-old friend, Kenny, in Battle Creek
breaking her leg on the wet gym floor
at the school across town where we bused her every day
our Mary
who has grown into a beautiful woman.
You listened   smiled   perhaps remembered
it doesn't matter
she's deep inside our very beings.

Words are not necessary to know it
remembering out loud or not.

The Hidden Inside

Though married over 50 years
you are newly deep inside me Lee.
How did this closeness happen?
What changes has the Alzheimer's caused?
Has it been our eyes
as we look at one another
intensely
long and steady
reaching far inside
to find one another
touch soul to soul
belong?
Gone are the years of stress
those
when we
each lived out our own dreams and visions.

We are together now
as we could only have hoped for
never dreamed possible.

Lovers

We are lovers
in that great sense of caring deeply for one another
intimately
as if no one else in the world matters.
We kiss
dance
hold hands
move together as if we are one
we are in love.

We leave past hopes
fears
anxieties
demands
behind that imaginary line
that marked the time
we first understood that
"Alzheimer's"
allows for no expectations.

What shall we do now
but
accept each other as we are
at this very moment
finding
it wonderful.

Loose Pants

I knew that you were losing weight
I knew that this was expected
Doctor Vogel told me early on
not to worry if you were overweight
"He'll need it down the road."
You've lost 20 pounds
since September.

It's December
two months such a little time
your pants hang loosely
your sleeves seem almost empty
you'll need the suspenders
that now lie in your drawer
to hold up your pants
too soon.
To know what will happen
is not the same
as seeing it happen.

I hold you tight
watching you go.

Time Has Passed

How much time has passed
since you entered Brewster Village?
Time enough
for you to have changed?
Were you once different
from now?
I need pictures to remind me.

The drifting
slowly changing
slipping away ever so slightly
makes me feel guilty
as if
I should have stopped it
and didn't
I want you back
maybe not to where you were
but at least
back to where you were
a year ago
three months ago

Do you too know
that you are going?

While Dying

Sometimes I wonder if you'd rather not talk at all
not have the phone ring
with someone hesitating to ask
"How are you?"
then mumbling something like
"I just wanted to hear your voice
for you to hear mine."
Would you rather die in quiet peace
alone
holding the daily paper
the signals of an ordinary day
even though unread?
Or do you want those faces
voices
knocks at the door
coming
to reassure you that you have been loved
will leave many behind
who will miss you.

After the Night

When I read the poems Lee
the ones about us   you and me
of those last few years when you were leaving
tears come to Libby's eyes.
Others lean forward   listen
tell me that it's good to share the stories
of the tenderness   hugs   singing down the halls
the big "HELLO'S" you shouted out
the loving of that time.
I'm not sure why it was so for us
the gentle peaceful time of your leaving
but I am grateful for memories:

Daniel, maybe eight years old playing dominoes
holding his head in his hands   waiting for your moves
Jim teasing you   causing you to burst into laughter
Christmas dinner with the Heywoods at Brewster
Ellen Kort on Valentine's Day bearing a big red heart
The whole church choir singing with you once more
The Bertschausen family sharing dinner with us
Fred bringing old pictures from Lawrence days together
Dale Duesing singing to you and everyone on your floor
Al in his big floppy hat with his book about pulp and paper
Marv with Lynn wearing a silly yellow cap made you laugh
Alice shopping for a birthday card you would sign
Mike from Alaska reminding you of playing recorders
with Camilla and Harold   the four of you.

How can we tell them that   inside   alone
because of their love
you were not alone.

Mourning

Lee,
friends tell me that they saw the picture
of Lib and Mary and me at the Queen Bee
having breakfast
just after you had passed away.
I feel embarrassed.
You had just died
an hour earlier
and there we were
eating eggs and pancakes
telling a reporter from the Post Crescent
about you
how you liked to eat at the Queen Bee
that we were hungry
after our night of saying good-by
wanted you with us in spirit
in a place you would want to be.

Rather than going home
mourning
quiet
solemn
appropriate
we needed a little more time
to absorb our loss
to be with you
in a place you often chose to be.

I think you'd understand.

Writing Doesn't Help

Putting down on paper
doesn't do what we're told it might.
Pain increases
memories leap to the front
sadness swells
a huge ache haunts the body
no release
no ridding   setting aside
occurs
when writing of the loss of
a mind.

Nevertheless
we try.